C000269622

Bible reflections
for older people

BRF
Ministries

BRF Ministries

15 The Chambers, Vineyard
Abingdon OX14 3FE
brf.org.uk

Bible Reading Fellowship is a charity (233280)
and company limited by guarantee (301324),
registered in England and Wales

ISBN 978 1 80039 253 3

Acknowledgements
Scripture quotations marked with the following abbreviations are taken from the version shown. Where
no abbreviation is given, the quotation is taken from the same version as the headline reference. NIV: The
Holy Bible, New International Version (Anglicised edition) copyright © 1979, 1984, 2011 by Biblica. Used by
permission of Hodder & Stoughton Publishers, a Hachette UK company. All rights reserved. 'NIV' is a registered
trademark of Biblica. UK trademark number 1448790. KJV: The Authorised Version of the Bible (The King James
Bible), the rights in which are vested in the Crown, are reproduced by permission of the Crown's Patentee,
Cambridge University Press. NRSV: The New Revised Standard Version of the Bible, Anglicised edition, copyright
© 1989, 1995 by the Division of Christian Education of the National Council of the Churches of Christ in the
United States of America. Used by permission. All rights reserved. GNT: the Good News Bible published by The
Bible Societies/HarperCollins Publishers Ltd, UK © American Bible Society 1966, 1971, 1976, 1992, used with
permission.

Every effort has been made to trace and contact copyright owners for material used in this resource. We
apologise for any inadvertent omissions or errors, and would ask those concerned to contact us so that full
acknowledgement can be made in the future.

A catalogue record for this book is available from the British Library

Printed and bound in the UK by Zenith Media NP4 0DQ

Contents

About the writers

Tony Horsfall is an author, retreat leader and mentor based in Bournemouth. He is the author of *Rhythms of Grace*, *Working From a Place of Rest* and *Grief Notes*. He is married to Jilly, a counsellor, and between them they have four children and six grandchildren. They are part of GodFirst Church and share a passion to see people thrive in life and ministry.

Valerie Eker is a retired teacher and a spiritual director, currently involved with a dynamic church on a housing estate with many social problems. It has come as a wonderful surprise that the last lap of life is as full of adventure as its earlier phases. She is sustained by her love of silence and prayer, a rich variety of friendships and frequent visits to her children and grandchildren.

'Tricia Williams is a freelance writer and editor with a passion for helping people engage with God's word. She has an interest in the spiritual support of those living with dementia and is the author of *God's Not Forgotten Me* (Cascade Books, 2022). She's married to Emlyn (also a writer for *Bible Reflections for Older People*) and has two children and a granddaughter.

David Butterfield was born in Yorkshire. After studying music, he felt the call to ordination in the Church of England. During his 40-year ministry, he served at churches in Southport, the Midlands and Shropshire. His final post was based at York Minster from which he retired in 2017. He and his wife Irene now live in Ripon in North Yorkshire. They have two adult children and one grandchild.

From the Editor

Welcome

Tim and Jean Howlett (see p. 34) try to go on retreat once a year. They also try to make Sundays different from other days, and they try not to be driven by 'oughts' but rather allow themselves space to listen for God's gentle call.

It's easy to become driven and rule-bound in our desire to do the right thing. Tim and Jean's quiet talk of 'trying' to do certain things, while not always managing to do them, is honest and faithful, the very opposite of rule-bound.

For many years I also made an annual retreat. There were suggestions rather than rules to help us listen for God's call. We would keep silence, we might pray a number of times in the day and we wouldn't read apart from the Bible passages suggested by the retreat director.

One evening, sitting at the broad bay window watching the sun dip over the North Sea, I noticed a young couple in difficulty. The boy slumped on the verge, seemingly the worse for wear, and the girl struggled to prop him up against a lamppost. A few moments later I saw another retreatant, Carla (p. 33), a retired doctor, slip out the front door and go over to the couple. She knelt beside them, took the boy's pulse and waited until someone came to take them home. She could have protected her silence; she chose the kinder, far more Christian way.

Go well

Using these reflections

Perhaps you have always had a special time each day for reading the Bible and praying. But now, as you grow older, you are finding it more difficult to keep to a regular pattern or find it harder to concentrate. Or, maybe you've never done this before. Whatever your situation, these Bible reflections aim to help you take a few moments to read God's Word and pray whenever you have time or feel that would be helpful.

When to read them

You might use these Bible reflections in the morning or last thing at night, but they work at any time of day. There are 40 reflections here, grouped around four themes, by four different writers. Each one includes some verses from the Bible, a reflection to help you in your own thinking about God, and a prayer suggestion. The reflections aren't dated, so it doesn't matter if you don't want to read every day. The Bible verses are printed, but you might prefer to follow them in your own Bible.

How to read them

- **Take time** to quieten yourself, becoming aware of God's presence, asking him to speak to you through the Bible and the reflection.

- **Read** the Bible verses and the reflection:
  - What do you especially like or find helpful in these verses?
  - What might God be saying to you through this reading?
  - Is there something to pray about or thank God for?

- **Pray.** Each reflection includes a prayer suggestion. You might like to pray for yourself or take the opportunity to think about and pray for others.

Hineni: Here I am

Tony Horsfall

I don't pretend to be a Hebrew scholar. Indeed, during my time at Bible College I was de-selected from the stream learning Hebrew and allocated to do Old Testament history instead. I managed Greek, but not Hebrew.

However, in this series of notes we will be giving close attention to a Hebrew word often used in the Bible. It is the word *hineni*, and it means 'Here I am'. It is the word often used as a response to God, and indicates an offering of oneself to him, a willingness to do his will. It suggests surrender, a response of love to the prior love of God.

In her *Sensible Shoes* series of novels, published by IVP, writer Sharon Garlough Brown has a character called Nathan Allen, an Old Testament professor who has the word *hineni* tattooed on his ankle to remind him of the fact that his life is given over to God.

Wherever we find ourselves on our journey through life, it is helpful to be reminded of the importance of surrender to God and willingness to embrace his will for our life no matter what that looks like.

Exodus 3:1–2a (NIV)

God in the ordinary

Now Moses was tending the flock of Jethro his father-in-law, the priest of Midian, and he led the flock to the far side of the wilderness and came to Horeb, the mountain of God. There the angel of the Lord appeared to him in flames of fire from within a bush.

Most days are ordinary days when we follow our normal routines and nothing special happens. Occasionally, though, we discover God is in the ordinary. It is as if heaven breaks through and we become conscious of God.

In this period of his life, Moses was working as a humble shepherd in an isolated part of the desert, perhaps feeling far away from God, neglected and forgotten. Yet that was not the case, and to grab his attention God speaks to him through the burning bush.

Maybe that is how you are feeling today? Perhaps you are isolated from friends and family, no longer able to attend church and cut off from fellowship. Or like Moses, you may be in a low period when life has become mundane, and you are simply going through the motions. Wherever we find ourselves today, and whatever our state of mind, God has not abandoned us and waits to break into this ordinary day.

■ **PRAYER**

Lord, help me become aware of your presence. May I recognise the signs of your nearness in the routine events of my life. Thank you that you will never leave me or forsake me. Amen

Exodus 3:2b–4a (NIV)

On being curious

Moses saw that though the bush was on fire it did not burn up. So Moses thought, 'I will go over and see this strange sight – why the bush does not burn up.' When the Lord saw that he had gone over to look, God called to him from within the bush, 'Moses! Moses!'

I live in a first-floor flat, and we have a lovely view over the busy road below. I love to sit at the window and watch what is happening. There is so much coming and going, traffic and people, and lots of interesting things to see. Perhaps I am naturally curious.

People say, 'Curiosity killed the cat,' but curiosity is a good thing. Without curiosity we would never learn, and many discoveries would not have been made. And in the spiritual life, being curious and wanting to know more about God is a good thing.

Moses was curious about the bush, and God used that to grab his attention. Moses noticed what was happening and went to see what was going on – he stepped forward. If we are to meet God in our ordinary days we must be alert and attentive, looking for signs of his presence and then being willing to respond to what we notice.

■ **PRAYER**

Lord, make me spiritually curious. Give me eyes to see where you are at work, and ears to hear what you are saying. I want to know you more. Amen

Exodus 3:4b–6a (NIV)

Holy ground

And Moses said, 'Here I am.' 'Do not come any closer,' God said, 'Take off your sandals, for the place where you are standing is holy ground.' Then he said, 'I am the God of your father, the God of Abraham, the God of Isaac and the God of Jacob.'

Do you remember being at school when the teacher took the class register? As names were called out, each pupil responded with, 'Here, miss.' 'Here, sir.'

Moses responds to God in a similar, but much deeper way. This is his *hineni* moment, when he realises who God is and responds accordingly. It is the God whom his ancestors worshipped, who now makes himself known to Moses. It is a moment of encounter, of recognition, of surrender. Moses becomes fully present to the presence of God.

He is asked to take off his shoes, a sign that he recognises the holiness of God. His shoes would have been dusty and dirty from traipsing round the desert as he tended the sheep. It is a symbolic act and speaks to us of the need to separate ourselves from anything unclean or unholy in our lives. It is also an expression of vulnerability, for shoes give us protection and bare feet are easily hurt or injured. However, before God we need not be afraid of being vulnerable. He deals with us gently, mercifully and always in love.

■ **PRAYER**

Lord, I pause to say, 'Here I am,' just as I am. Amen

1 Samuel 3:1–3 (NIV, abridged)

God in the night

The boy Samuel ministered before the Lord under Eli... One night Eli, whose eyes were becoming so weak that he could barely see, was lying down in his usual place. The lamp of God had not yet gone out, and Samuel was lying down in the house of the Lord, where the ark of God was.

This story takes me back to the days of my childhood, growing up in a Yorkshire mining village and attending the local Methodist chapel. There we were encouraged to memorise scripture by heart, and this was one of the passages we were given to learn.

Samuel, whose name means 'heard by God', was born as a gift from God to his mother Hannah, who had been barren. From a young age he was given back to God and was under the care of the elderly priest Eli in the sanctuary at Shiloh. There he helped in whatever practical ways he could, sweeping the floors, lighting candles, tidying up.

It was nighttime, and everything is quiet as Eli and Samuel prepare to sleep. This is the moment that God chooses to speak, when all is still and the place is silent. I often find that God speaks to me during the night, as if the daytime is too busy for God to get through. Only when I am still can I hear his gentle whisper.

■ **PRAYER**

Lord, speak to me, even in the night. Amen

1 Samuel 3:4–5 (NIV)

Recognising the voice

Then the Lord called Samuel. Samuel answered, 'Here I am.' And he ran to Eli and said, 'Here I am; you called me.' But Eli said, 'I did not call; go back and lie down.' So he went and lay down.

How do you respond to being woken in the middle of the night? Most of us are a little grumpy if our sleep is disturbed by noisy neighbours, loud motorbikes or dogs barking.

Being apprenticed to Eli, the young boy Samuel learned how to be a servant. He loved to be helpful, and his attitude was one of joyful anticipation of ways in which he could please, even in the middle of the night. When he hears someone call his name, he assumes it is Eli, and he runs to see how he can help.

Samuel did not yet know the Lord and did not recognise it was the voice of God (v. 7). Most of us are slow to recognise when God is speaking to us. We tend to think it is our imagination, assuming that God would never speak to us; but in so doing we miss the moment, for God speaks more often than we realise, and to each one of us.

Don't be surprised if God speaks to you, either through scripture or in the quietness of your own heart. He loves to communicate with his people.

■ **PRAYER**

Lord, I pray for the ability to recognise your voice. Amen

1 Samuel 3:8b–10 (NIV, abridged)

Speak, Lord

Then Eli realised that the Lord was calling the boy. So Eli told Samuel, 'Go and lie down, and if he calls you, say, "Speak, Lord, for your servant is listening"... The Lord came and stood there, calling as at the other times, 'Samuel! Samuel!' Then Samuel said, 'Speak, for your servant is listening.'

We don't always understand things straight away, do we? Often, we are slow to catch on and need things explained more than once.

After being disturbed by Samuel for a third time, Eli at last recognises this must be God. His advice is sound and full of wisdom. The best thing is to wait for God to speak again, for he surely will; and then to respond with open ears to what he has to say.

Samuel seems to have had *hineni* written on his heart. He does not actually use the words 'Here I am' this time, but it is the essence of his response. He is making himself available for whatever God wants him to do. He is all ears when it comes to doing the will of God, and just as he ran obediently to Eli, so now he dedicates himself wholeheartedly to obeying God. Samuel would go on to become one of the greatest of the prophets.

■ **PRAYER**

Lord, I too am your servant. Here I am, ready to do your will. I yield myself to you. Amen

Isaiah 6:1–3 (NIV, abridged)

I saw the Lord

In the year that king Uzziah died, I saw the Lord, high and exalted, seated on a throne; and the train of his robe filled the temple. Above him were seraphim… And they were calling to one another: 'Holy, holy, holy is the Lord Almighty; the whole earth is full of his glory.'

When Queen Elizabeth II died in September 2022, it was a sad moment in Britain. Ten days of mourning enabled people to express their sense of loss at the passing of this much-loved monarch. Perhaps there was a similar feel in Israel when Uzziah died, about 740BC. He was not perfect, but his reign had brought peace and prosperity.

Isaiah enters the temple at this important juncture, probably to pray for the nation, but sees instead an amazing vision of the glory and majesty of God, the true sovereign and eternal King. It is a vivid reminder that while earthly rulers pass away, there is no need to fear for God remains in control.

Sometimes things change in our lives, too, and we enter times of instability and uncertainty. Loved ones pass away, perhaps we move house, our health fails and so on. We feel shaken and at a loss. That is when we need to remind ourselves that God does not change, and we are in the grip of his grace.

■ PRAYER

Lord, I am so grateful that you are still on the throne. Steady my heart today. Amen

Isaiah 6:5 (NIV)

Unclean lips

'Woe to me!' I cried. 'I am ruined! For I am a man of unclean lips, and I live among a people of unclean lips, and my eyes have seen the King, the Lord Almighty.'

Late on in his life, Uzziah was made unclean through leprosy. Isaiah perceives that the nation and himself are no better, for their words have made them unclean too. His encounter with the thrice holy God exposes his own sinfulness, for which he repents.

Nowadays most people swear, and foul talk is everywhere. It is almost impossible to watch a film or TV programme that is not full of expletives, and for some people their ordinary conversation is littered with four-letter words. Even the name of God is commonly taken in vain.

Our speech can also be spoilt by lying, half-truths, gossip, slander, innuendo, exaggeration and so on. Of course, sometimes we sin by what we do not say, failing to speak out against such things as injustice, racism, bullying and inequality. Either way, we know it is not easy to tame the tongue and all of us need the cleansing of God on our lips. Thankfully, because of the death of Jesus on the cross, forgiveness is readily available.

■ PRAYER

Lord, forgive me when my words dishonour you or my silence allows sin to flourish. Cleanse my lips and make me whole. Let my words be gracious and full of kindness. Amen

Isaiah 6:8–9 (NIV)

Who will go?

Then I heard the voice of the Lord saying, 'Whom shall I send? And who will go for us?' And I said, 'Here I am. Send me!' He said, 'Go and tell this people: "Be ever hearing, but never understanding; be ever seeing, but never perceiving."'

Testimony is a powerful witness to the grace of God, and each of us has a story to tell. Isaiah writes in the first person, sharing from his own experience of surrender to the will of God. His vision in the temple was for him a *hineni* moment, when he feels compelled to offer himself to God again, even though he is already a prophet.

Notice that God, who is sovereign and rules over all, still looks for people to partner with him. He chooses frail human beings to be his messengers, even though he could use angels. Why? Because angels have no testimony of forgiveness and grace as human beings have. Only those who have known forgiveness personally, like Isaiah, can tell others where grace and mercy can be found.

You may feel your days of being 'sent' are over, but there are many ways in which we can serve God, even when we are confined and restricted. We can pray, and we can speak words of kindness and good news to those we meet. Sometimes 'being' is just as important as doing.

■ PRAYER
Lord, use me, as I am, where I am. Amen

Hebrews 10:5b–7 (NIV)

Delighted in God

'Sacrifice and offerings you did not desire, but a body you prepared for me; with burnt offerings and sin offerings you were not pleased. Then I said, "Here I am – it is written about me in the scroll – I have come to do your will, my God."'

The writer of Hebrews places these words from the Old Testament (Psalm 40:6–8) in the mouth of Jesus, as they perfectly describe both his coming into the world and his going to the cross. At both his incarnation and his crucifixion, Jesus said to his Father, 'Here I am (*hineni*).' His surrender to God's will is the supreme example of the response we have been thinking about.

First, he said 'Yes' to God by taking a human body and entering our world, being born as a babe at Bethlehem. Then he said 'Yes' to God by offering that very body as the once-for-all-time sacrifice for our sins, choosing to do the will of God even though it meant the ultimate sacrifice.

The best response we can ever make to such love is to say to him in turn, 'Here I am.' It is to place ourselves completely at his disposal and allow him to shape our lives and direct our paths, and then to live contentedly with whatever he chooses for us.

■ PRAYER

Lord, the best place to be is in the centre of your will. I surrender to your love. Amen

Giving and receiving

Valerie Eker

I wonder if you consider yourself to be more a giver or a receiver?

We often say it is more blessed to give than to receive, and it is. There is always satisfaction to be found in giving, whether it is a present, a helping hand or just a smile. Anything given in love blesses both the giver and the receiver.

As we get older, we may find ourselves able to do less than we used to do and be more dependent on other people. There are still things we can give to others, but the way we receive what they give to us is a way of giving in itself. If we do not receive well what another offers to us, we rob them of the joy of being a giver and we devalue their gift.

In this series we look closely at what God gives to us and our need to offer him our thanks and to use his gifts well. We also reflect on how God looks at us and how he values the gifts we offer to him and to one another.

There might be one or two surprises here.

John 3:16 (NIV)

The gift of eternal life

For God so loved the world that he gave his one and only Son, that whoever believes in him shall not perish but have eternal life.

One Christmas in childhood, I was delighted to be given a small torch in my stocking. I loved shining it into murky corners or using it to find my way in the dark. Best of all, it enabled me to carry on reading secretly under the blankets when I was sent up to bed. Of course, the inevitable happened, and one day the battery ran out. The only way I could read in bed was if I had a lamp that was plugged into the mains. This helps me understand how amazing God's gift of eternal life is.

At birth, we are given the precious gift of human life. Truly, we are wonderfully made. Yet, however long or short our life, we know that one day it will run out. The apostle John tells us that in the beginning, Jesus was with God and he was God (John 1:1). His life is eternal life: the kind which never dies. So, when we receive him, we are given his own kind of life and it is like being plugged into the mains.

Although our bodies wear out, we ourselves continue living eternally in him.

■ PRAYER

Lord, thank you for your gift of eternal life. Please fill us with your life today. Amen

Galatians 5:22–23 (NIV)

The gift of a fruitful life

The fruit of the Spirit is love, joy, peace, forbearance, kindness, goodness, faithfulness, gentleness and self-control. Against such things there is no law.

If I had the spirit of Beethoven living in me, I would be able to compose symphonies like his. If I had the spirit of Shakespeare living in me, I could write plays like a genius. Of course, they are both dead and buried and there is no way they could take up residence in me.

Yet Jesus told his disciples that it would be good for them if he went away, because then he could gift his spirit to them, forever. He was offering not only to be with them, but to live in them and through them.

He said he could gradually enable them from the inside to resist temptation; to know and speak the truth; to forgive the unforgiveable; to be compassionate and merciful; to love all people, even the unlovely.

We too are offered this astonishing gift of having the very nature of Jesus Christ planted in us. It may begin as a tiny seed, but over time it grows and ripens until our nature is transformed into his likeness. It is a lifetime's work, but the end goal is that there should be many 'little Christs' showing his character to the world.

■ PRAYER

Lord, I am so unlike you now, but I ask you to come in and change me from the inside out. Amen

John 14:6 (NIV)

The gift of a way

Jesus said, 'I am the way and the truth and the life. No one comes to the Father except through me.'

In our local shopping centre there are three lifts and a flight of stairs. When I have finished doing my shopping, I can choose whether to lug it up the stairs to my car or to stand in the lift and be carried up. Guess which I normally choose.

It speaks to me of what Jesus has done for us and why he told us to remain in him. It is as if God has created a lift shaft from heaven to the basement of life. Jesus is like the lift in the shaft. He has travelled the whole journey of life most perfectly on our behalf: from heaven down to earth, in total obedience to his Father, through death, then back up to heaven again.

No matter how hard we try, we cannot by our own efforts rise to be united to God. Yet, we can be baptised into Christ and in him be lifted into God's presence.

It does not matter how low we have fallen; in him we can make the journey upwards and live forever with God. The ground rule of being a Christian is to lay aside our own efforts to please God and to abide in Christ, who has done everything for us.

■ PRAYER
Here I am, Lord. Please receive me into yourself and hold me there. Amen

Matthew 10:8b (NIV)

Giving forwards

'Freely you have received, freely give.'

During a time in my life when I hadn't a bean to my name, I needed some very expensive legal advice. On finding this out, some friends offered to pay it for me. 'Oh no. I can't possibly let you do that,' I protested. 'I can't pay you back.' 'We know,' they responded, 'but one day you may be able to pay it forward.'

This was new to me. They explained that they had once received an extravagant gift of a lot of money with instructions to 'pay it forward to someone else when you can'. I was that someone. So, I accepted their gift and have since been able to 'pay it forward' myself.

It illustrates perfectly what Jesus meant when he reminded the disciples that his gift to them of eternal life was a free gift – one for which they could never pay him back. His only condition was that what he had given freely to them, they were to pass on equally freely to other people. He had welcomed them into his kingdom. They must welcome others. He had forgiven them all their sin. They must forgive others when they were offended against. He had given them everything: a good measure, pressed down to overflowing (see Luke 6:38). They too must be generous givers.

■ **PRAYER**

Lord, thank you for your astonishing gift of eternal life to us. Help us to pass it on freely to others. Amen

2 Timothy 1:6–7 (NIV, abridged)

The gift of the Holy Spirit

Fan into flame the gift of God, which is in you through the laying on of my hands. For the Spirit God gave us does not make us timid, but gives us power, love and self-discipline.

Each morning in winter, my mother got up early to light a fire so that we could dress by its warmth. She cleared the grate of debris left from yesterday's fire, putting aside any still useful pieces of coal. She laid tightly twisted circles of newspaper on top of loosely crumpled sheets. The little reusable bits were scattered over with small shards of kindling wood. Finally, fresh coal was carefully arranged to sit lightly on top.

We watched as she lit a match and held it under her construction. To encourage the first flickering flames to be fanned into fire, she quickly opened a double page spread of newspaper and held it tightly across the opening of the fireplace. This allowed an updraught of air which set the whole thing ablaze.

God has given us the flame of his Spirit as a gift. We have to fan it into fire. So, find space to be still in God's presence. Shut out the world. Be touched by his love. Offer it back to him in worship and thanksgiving. Bask in his love. Let its warmth flow through you and out to others in acts of kindness.

■ PRAYER

Lord, thank you for the gift of your Holy Spirit. May he burn brightly in us today. Amen

Ephesians 5:20 (KJV)

Giving thanks

Giving thanks always for all things unto God and the Father in the name of our Lord Jesus Christ.

Choosing and giving a gift can be quite an art form. Ideally, we match the gift to the tastes or needs of the person we are giving it to. Once we have given it, our joy is completed when we see (or hear about) the pleasure our gift has given.

While we don't give in order to receive anything in return, receiving thanks somehow strengthens the bond between the giver and the receiver. When Jesus healed ten lepers, they were all delighted but only one returned to thank him. Even Jesus noticed something was missing: 'Were not all ten cleansed? Where are the other nine? Has no one returned to give praise to God except this foreigner?' (Luke 17:17–18, NIV).

Although God's gift of healing had been a free gift, they still owed God a debt of gratitude. If we have to remind ourselves to thank other people when they have given us something, let's not forget to give God thanks for all he gives us, from the air we breathe to the beauty in creation; a roof over our heads; food and friends and so much more.

The more you give thanks, the more you will realise how much you have to give thanks for. Not only that, as your gratitude grows, so will your contentment.

■ **PRAYER**

Father, forgive us for taking so much for granted. Thank you for…
(insert your own thoughts here). Amen

Luke 21:1–4 (NIV, abridged)

Giving from the heart

[Jesus] saw the rich putting their gifts into the temple treasury. He also saw a poor widow put in two very small copper coins. 'Truly I tell you,' he said, 'this poor widow has put in more than all the others. All these people gave their gifts out of their wealth; but she out of her poverty put in all she had to live on.'

Jesus had been teaching his disciples not to be impressed by the Pharisees' showy displays of righteousness, done to win the admiration of other people.

By contrast, he points out a poor widow who quietly offers to God all that she has. In that offering she shows a great love of God and a desire to please him from her heart. I imagine her trying to hide and be anonymous out of shame for giving so little and for fear of condemnation from the Pharisees.

Yet Jesus judges by a different scale of values and sees more worth in her than in the ones who poured in masses of money so conspicuously. Knowing that God looks at our hearts and what we think and do secretly, let's examine our own attitudes to giving and perhaps make adjustments in the light of this story.

■ **PRAYER**

Lord Jesus, you gave the whole of yourself to God for our sakes.
Please give us the grace to give equally generously to you. Amen

Mark 13:11 (NIV)

The gift of the right word

'Whenever you are arrested and brought to trial, do not worry beforehand about what to say. Just say whatever is given you at the time, for it is not you speaking, but the Holy Spirit.'

In John 8, a woman had been caught in the very act of adultery. Triumphantly, the Pharisees marched her through the watching crowds towards Jesus. They wanted to trap him. If Jesus was really committed to upholding the law of Moses, they thought he would have the woman stoned to death. How then would people believe in his gospel of love? If he let her off, they would accuse him of failing to keep the law, so demonstrating he could not be the Son of God.

They watched and waited while Jesus drew in the dust.

I believe he was listening deeply, inwardly, to God.

'Father, what shall I say? Give me the right words.'

When he looked up, he said, 'Let any one of you who is without sin be the first to throw a stone at her.'

One by one the accusers shrank back and withdrew. Very simply, Jesus caught them out. Later he told his disciples, if they were put on trial, not to worry beforehand what they should say. He promised the Holy Spirit would give them exactly the right words they needed.

We too can receive this gift if we listen inwardly to God.

■ **PRAYER**

Father, please give us the words you want us to speak. Amen

Matthew 14:15–20 (NIV, abridged)

The gift of multiplication

The disciples came to him and said... 'Send the crowds away, so that they can go to the villages and buy themselves some food.' Jesus replied... 'You give them something to eat.' 'We have here only five loaves of bread and two fish,' they answered. 'Bring them here to me,' he said... Taking the five loaves and two fish and looking up to heaven, he gave thanks and broke the loaves. Then he gave them to the disciples, and the disciples gave them to the people. They all ate and were satisfied.

'Use your common sense', my head teacher often said.

She would have been pleased with the disciples. They saw the hunger of the crowds and asked Jesus to do the common-sense thing: 'Send the people away to buy food.'

Immediately, Jesus asked them to feed the crowds. Humanly, it was an impossible task. The disciples felt totally inadequate. So Jesus told them to give him whatever they had, however tiny it was. He took their gift, offered it to God and multiplied it abundantly. Then he returned it to them so they could complete their task.

God seems to delight in asking us to do things for which we feel inadequate. It forces us to turn to him for help so that he can work with and through us. He takes the little we have, then turns it into something so much greater than we could have made it by ourselves.

■ **PRAYER**

Lord, here I am, feeling so small. Please take me as I am and use me to your glory. Amen

John 12:25 (NIV)

What you give away is what you keep

'Anyone who loves their life will lose it, while anyone who hates their life in this world will keep it for eternal life.'

Jesus has sometimes been heralded as 'the man who turned the world upside down' and so he is.

Normally, we cling to life and do everything in our power to avoid death.

Strangely, Jesus tells us to 'die' in order to live. By that he meant that we should be willing to lay down our lives in service to him and to one another. It means dying to selfishness.

There have been people in every generation who have taken Jesus seriously and discovered they have never been happier than when giving themselves away in his service. Not only that, but the more we give ourselves away, the more like him we become. We gain a character like his, though we may not see this ourselves.

Because he has made us, we all have something we can give to others. It might be some practical help or a word of encouragement; a cup of tea or a listening ear; some help with finances or just a smile. Whatever is given with love enriches the one who gives and the one who receives.

■ PRAYER

Dear Lord, thank you for giving yourself to us. Give us the grace to follow your example. Show us how you want us to give ourselves to you today. Amen

The Gift of Years

 Debbie Thrower is the pioneer of BRF's Anna Chaplaincy for Older People ministry, offering spiritual care to older people, and is widely involved in training and advocacy. Visit **annachaplaincy.org. uk** to find out more.

Debbie writes...

Welcome!

I'm excited to dive into this issue as it features some of my favourite people and topics that are dear to me. Tim and Jean Howlett have been Anna Chaplaincy supporters since my earliest days at BRF. They have come on our training courses, joined the network and persevered in spreading the word of Anna Chaplaincy in their part of the home counties for years. What's more, the couple are always the first to send an encouraging note and promise to be praying for you.

A spiritual dividend of more people than ever in retirement is many choosing to spend time volunteering or using gifts in other ways. I applaud those featured in our notes finding a sense of purpose through writing. I'm keen to read 'Tricia Williams' insights, for example, on a perennial spiritual problem – the lack of forgiveness.

My son is called Samuel because I've always loved the Old Testament story of the young boy Samuel responding to that mysterious voice calling him with the words, 'Here I am.' What a fine quality, to be alert when the master calls and willing to serve. We're sure to gain a great deal from Tony Horsfall's focus on the loving call of God, whatever our age.

Debbie

Go for it! Writing in later life

Judith and John Lampard are well known in Methodist and ecumenical circles. Judith grew up in Derbyshire village Methodism and has been a Methodist local preacher for over 40 years. John qualified as a solicitor before being ordained as a Methodist minister and has served in the north of England, in the south and since 1985 in different parts of London, where he retired in 2006. They are both as busy in retirement as in their 'working' years: writing, speaking and preaching, active in their local community, nurturing an allotment and enjoying the company of their six grandchildren. Amid all this, they have both carved out the time to complete significant writing projects: John his grandfather's biography, *John Lampard of India*, and Judith two booklets about women whose stories 'cried out for justice': Martha Hall, the sister of John Wesley, and Mary Vazeille, aka Molly Wesley, his wife.

For John, his retirement plans always included this book, a true labour of love: 'It really dates back to 1972,' he says, 'when my father died, and I suddenly realised I was cut off from whole areas of family history. There was this great sense of not knowing anything about the past. I knew virtually nothing about my grandfather, apart from the fact that he had been in India as a missionary. My father was born there and left to come to this country when he was about twelve or thirteen and he never went back.'

Very slowly, John started piecing together what his grandfather did in India, digging deep in Salvation Army and Methodist archives, mainly available online. He even found two of his grandfather's diaries. Year after year, progress was slow and bitty until suddenly everything changed: 'When Covid came, I thought it was now or never and that gave me the space to knit it all together into a coherent biography.'

His son-in-law, Steve, put it into book form and organised the printing of 100 high-quality copies, mainly for family and friends. Judith's projects have had a much shorter timeline: 'When I started volunteering at Wesley's Chapel, I looked closely at John Wesley's grave. There's this wonderful long eulogy about him on the front of the monument and then on one side it just says, 'Also Mrs Martha Hall, sister of John Wesley 1706–1791', and I thought how horrible for any woman, that she should just be a sister when she was buried, with nothing about her life. I felt really strongly that I wanted to know more about her and let her story come out.'

Judith also made good use of online archives, but one of the most fruitful sources of information was a stay at Gladstone's Library in Hawarden, Flintshire. 'I spent practically all the time reading pamphlets and booklets, and also biographies of other people, to glean snippets about Martha's life and times: things that her mother and siblings had said about her, for example. It took a long time to gather material but there was a moment when I felt I had enough to begin to try and draft something. Martha had this terrible, terrible marriage. She was thrown out of the house, her husband was totally unfaithful yet, remarkably, she looked after the woman who had his baby and gave her money. Her brother Charles said, "You shouldn't be doing that." And she said, "Oh, I should, because it's not her fault and nobody is going to take any pity on her whereas anybody would take pity on me."

'There was the assumption in some books that because Martha had been to events arranged by Samuel Johnson, that it must have been her brothers, John and Charles, who arranged for her to go, and it was so nice to find the snippet in which Johnson said to her, "Do bring your brother…"'

One of the most exciting moments for Judith came near the end of her research. 'I found out that Emeritus Professor John Walsh in Oxford had discovered five letters that referred to Martha and nobody seemed to have picked them up. They were letters from her niece, Sarah, to a friend of both of them, talking about John Wesley's death and how Martha has reacted to it, and about Martha's own death and the funeral. It was just so exciting. I sent a copy of the booklet to Professor Walsh and had the nicest email back from his wife saying how he was pleased that I was using his work. That's when it felt really worth doing: to have joined up what he had found with other pieces of the jigsaw and help bring the whole thing to life. I also found the original memorial which had been on Martha's grave, which included these words, "She opened her mouth with wisdom, and in her tongue was the law of kindness" (Proverbs 31:26). Sadly, during later renovations to the vault, the quote was removed so the words are no longer there.'

So what advice would John and Judith give to other people who may be contemplating a writing project in retirement?

'Go for it!' says John. 'If you don't do it, nothing will happen. Still nothing may happen, but go for it. You might regret it if you don't, and it's amazing what you can do in your later years.'

Judith agrees: 'Certainly I would say get started. My temptation would have been to say where am I going to find enough time to do it, but as it worked out, I kept finding little bits of information and little bits of time, and gradually built up the story. So I'm very grateful to have got started and made the time along the way.'

For further information about John and Judith's books, please contact the editor: **eley.mcainsh@brf.org.uk**.

A poem to mark the joyful turning point between winter and spring...

 Carla McCowen is a retired consultant paediatrician. She lives in Wensleydale and has written poetry on and off throughout her adult life. She published *The Call of the Curlew* in 2011, illustrating many of the poems herself. She is a spiritual director and enjoys singing with the Ripon Choral Society.

Equinox

Yesterday winter's steely grip held the land
the heavy sky merged
with the high moor
where dark lines of walls
sheltered drifts of snow;
lonely sheep tugged
at the withered grass
no bird sang
only the high call of the curlew
pleaded for the unimaginable Spring.

Today the gentle fingers of the sun
caress the iron earth; bare trees, their buds wine red
cast blue shadows
on the hoary grass
little birds dart and chatter
a blackbird sings.
The world is poised
waiting to surrender
to the inexorable embrace of Spring.

From *The Call of the Curlew* by Carla McCowen. Used with kind permission.

Meet the Howletts

Tim and Jean Howlett have been stalwarts of the Anna Chaplaincy network from its earliest days. They were both brought up within Christian families, Tim in Northampton and Jean on the Wirral. They met 58 years ago at a Christian Endeavour holiday home and they celebrate their 56th anniversary this year. 'They say holiday romances don't last,' says Jean, 'well, we prove they do!'

Tim and Jean became deeply involved in working with older people after Tim took early retirement from his role as a social worker. Jean takes up the story: 'There was a couple at our church in Aylesbury who said, "We think you might be interested in coming to this meeting." It was called the Caleb Challenge and it was about working with older people. That's how the vision of working with older people was planted.'

A few years later, a seemingly chance encounter with BRF's Karen Laister at a Christian retailers and suppliers retreat led to an introduction to the embryonic Anna Chaplaincy. They had been frustrated at the lack of resources for ministry with older people, 'but Karen said, "I'll take your details. BUT JUST HOLD ON. There is something happening at BRF", and that really was the acorn.

'Soon after that we had a little email from Debbie Thrower to say, "We've got your names, we'll be in touch." So really we've been with Anna Chaplaincy from even before the beginning. We've been to several conferences and retreats and at one retreat in Poole, which Debbie was leading, Tim and I ended up on a table on our own at lunchtime. Debbie came and sat with us and started chatting about The Gift of Years [the original name of the ministry] and by the end of the conversation we just knew that that was where we would receive our source of help. I mean, obviously our help comes from God, but also through this group. It was brilliant. Absolutely brilliant.' Tim adds, 'We've always felt we wanted to identify with Anna Chaplaincy, almost as a recognition of our sense of calling to work with older people. It's giving us the training and the tools and the resources to do the work well, and more than that, it's giving us fellowship too. It's like a family.'

What is mine to do?

For anyone committed to working with and supporting older people, it would be easy to take on an all-consuming workload, and Tim and Jean are no exception. How do they balance the needs of others with their own need for rest and self-care? 'One of the things that we do try to do is have a retreat sometime during the year,' says Jean, 'For example, one year we attended Martha's Day Out with Anna Chaplaincy's Debbie Ducille, and that was absolutely amazing. It left us with a key question: *What is mine to do?* And therefore, what is not mine to do? We need to discern what to let go of and what to carry on doing. The other thing which is key is to know your limitations. God has given us gifts, and he doesn't want us to go outside of these gifts. He wants us to know these gifts and to use them.'

Their understanding has evolved as they've got older themselves. 'We are setting time aside,' says Tim, 'whereas we perhaps didn't in the past. But one thing we've always held on to is Sunday. There are certain things we try not to do on a Sunday, mainly more practical things – chores and errands – and so we do try to find that time of rest.' Jean finds the image of a rose is helpful when thinking of these things:

'Just as a rose gradually opens up, we open up, gradually becoming wiser about Jesus and about what he really wants us to do and wants us to be. Balance, self-care, sabbath and restoration are all interlinked with each other, and above all linked to Jesus at the centre.

'We used to live in a state that was dominated by "oughts": we constantly expected ourselves to do as much as we could. But now we've learned to lean on Jesus, to withdraw slightly and say, "God, what do you want us to do?" And then the important thing is to wait for God's leading.

'In Exodus 33:14 (NIV) it says, "My Presence will go with you, and I will give you rest."

'One truth remains for us: the Lord is with us! Simply because of his great love and care, God has promised to remain with us. As we choose to trust in him, we too can experience his peace and rest.'

Forgiveness

'Tricia Williams

Forgiveness: what a wonderful word. Whether given or received, forgiveness brings to each one of us a transforming freedom, a sense of a fresh start. But often, it doesn't feel that simple. There's our anxiety and guilt, the unwillingness to recognise our sin, the struggle to forgive others and the pain of living with unforgiveness.

As we grow older, it can sometimes feel as if we are dragging an increasing load of regrets, mistakes and sin – from distant memories and from those things we are now no longer able to resolve ourselves. Praise God that – as disciples of Jesus – we can say 'thank you' that we *are* forgiven through *his* death and resurrection. It's one thing to know this in theory, but another to work it out in our living, perhaps especially at this stage of our lives.

Over the coming days, we'll look at some key Bible passages, especially from the gospels and epistles, to help us think again about this receiving and giving of forgiveness. Let's come to God's word with a prayerful, open heart, ready to hear the gentle whisper of his Spirit. Jesus says: 'Come to me, all you who are weary and burdened, and I will give you rest' (Matthew 11:28, NIV).

Isaiah 53:4–5 (NIV)

Amazing grace

Surely he took up our pain and bore our suffering, yet we considered him punished by God, stricken by him, and afflicted. But he was pierced for our transgressions, he was crushed for our iniquities; the punishment that brought us peace was on him, and by his wounds we are healed.

John was in a reflective mood as we spoke together. He'd had a career in the armed services and knew that he had hurt many people. 'I've wasted my life,' he said. Surely, God wasn't interested in the likes of him. But here, in these words of scripture, we find amazing grace and truth about God.

He knows each one of us. Yet, he sent his Son, Jesus, to die for us. Now, we can be at peace with God, knowing that we *are* forgiven through his death, restored into relationship with him by his sacrifice. And notice, it's not just our 'transgressions' but it's our pain and suffering that Jesus carried on the cross too. Past 'sin' leaves deep regret, and hurts run like scars through our lives. God's word assures us that it doesn't need to be this way: 'By his wounds we are healed.'

Read these words of scripture again, reflecting on what Jesus' death means for you.

■ PRAYER

'Amazing Grace! How sweet the sound, that saved a wretch like me…' (John Newton, 1725–1807). Bring the burdens of your sin and pain to God. Receive his healing. Thank him that, in Jesus, you are forgiven.

Romans 8:1–2 (NIV)

No condemnation

Therefore, there is now no condemnation for those who are in Christ Jesus, because through Christ Jesus the law of the Spirit who gives life has set you free from the law of sin and death.

Sometimes our problem is not that we refuse to forgive others, or that they refuse to forgive us – but that we can't forgive ourselves. Through life's journey, our self-pride takes a hit as we learn that we are *not* perfect – and that can hurt.

But there's good news. Even though I might judge and condemn myself, God does not. Instead, he leads me to the cross and shows me Jesus who died for my sin, who was raised to life again and gives me his Spirit, enabling me to live in him. It's done. Christ's forgiveness is 'once for all' (Hebrews 10:10), and there is *nothing* that can separate me from the love of God in Christ Jesus (Romans 8:38–39). Who am I to disagree with God?

Being aware of our own unworthiness before God is, of course, a good corrective to our human pride; but preoccupation with our past failings can prevent us from enjoying the life in Christ which he has given. He has set us free 'from the law of sin and death' to serve him. Let's do that today.

■ **PRAYER**

'Thanks be to God! He gives us the victory through our Lord Jesus Christ' (1 Corinthians 15:57). Amen

1 John 1:9 (NIV)

If we confess...

If we confess our sins, he is faithful and just and will forgive us our sins and purify us from all unrighteousness.

If Christ has done it all, doesn't that mean I can simply forget about my sins and get on with my life? Why then are we troubled when we knowingly think, say or do wrong? There is something else here in these words of scripture.

We know that in Christ's death on the cross he took the punishment for our sin. Yet, day by day, as frail human beings, we still get things wrong. Frequently, the Holy Spirit alerts us to a harshly spoken word or an unkind thought. Unacknowledged, a shadow creeps across our relationship with holy God. Perhaps you are aware of unconfessed sin in your own life and it's troubling you in this way.

Scripture and church liturgy bring help and encouragement in confessing our sins regularly before God and one another (e.g. James 5:16). The ways in which we might do this are not a condition of our salvation; but the recognition of our unworthiness before God – 'all have sinned' (Romans 3:23) – enables us to come to him in repentance and to receive his certain forgiveness. Take time to reflect now, and then, if you feel able, confess your sin to God and make the words of this prayer your own.

■ **PRAYER**

'Most merciful God… Forgive us our sins, heal us by your Spirit and raise us to new life in Christ. Amen'*

* Church of England Common Worship Night Prayer

Psalm 103:8, 11–12 (NIV)

Deep and wide

The Lord is compassionate and gracious, slow to anger, abounding in love… For as high as the heavens are above the earth, so great is his love for those who fear him; as far as the east is from the west, so far has he removed our transgressions from us.

Sometimes, in the depths of night, unable to sleep, we remember past sin, and we almost can't believe (or *feel*) that we are truly forgiven. Reflect on these words of David, the psalmist. He had plenty of sins to remember (e.g. sleeping with Bathsheba, 2 Samuel 11). Yet, he knew that he was forgiven by his Father. His sin was dealt with by a compassionate and gracious God who loves his children.

'As far as the east is from the west.' Think about it. The separation from our sin is infinity. God forgives us – 'It is finished.' There is an assumption about our relationship with God in these words – 'those who fear him.' Yet, there is also growing hope and blessing caught up in our knowledge of God. As we turn to him, aware of our 'transgressions', we come to know his love and forgiveness.

In response to God's forgiveness, the psalmist's 'guilt-riddenness' is replaced with praise (v. 22).

■ PRAYER

'Praise the Lord, my soul, and forget not all his benefits – who forgives all your sins and heals all your diseases, who redeems your life from the pit and crowns you with love and compassion' (Psalm 103:2–4). Amen

Mark 2:5, 11–12a (NIV)

Healed

When Jesus saw their faith, he said to the paralysed man, 'Son, your sins are forgiven... I tell you, get up, take up your mat and go home.' He got up, took his mat and walked out in full view of them all. This amazed everyone and they praised God.

'Yes, I have peace with God,' Jill tells me out of the depths of her dementia and the armchair from which she cannot move unaided. Like the paralysed man – and for many of us I suspect – the physical problems we live with are not the main reason for having or not having inner peace.

The obvious need of the paralysed man in these verses was his inability to walk. So why did Jesus go first to forgiveness? His words raised another question for the religious leaders. Surely, only God can forgive sins (v. 7)? The man's physical problems might have been obvious to everyone, but Jesus, Son of God, knew there was a bigger issue.

In our own lives, disability or sickness may be a means of bringing praise to God – as with this paralysed man. Yet, it is his healing alongside certain forgiveness that gave him the strength to get up and walk with God. Jesus, God's Son, knows us through and through, and offers us deep cure of our sin – that's the amazing miracle.

■ **PRAYER**

Lord Jesus, I thank and praise you for your work in my life. Help me to serve you today in the strength you give. Amen

Matthew 18:21–22 (NIV)

Forgiving others

Then Peter came to Jesus and asked, 'Lord, how many times shall I forgive my brother or sister who sins against me? Up to seven times?' Jesus answered, 'I tell you, not seven times, but seventy-seven times.'

'I can never forgive him,' Ellen said. She wasn't talking minor, distant wrongs, but about decades of continual abuse. Through a difficult marriage, her faith had sustained her. Now, nearing the end of life, she expressed this hurt. These words of Jesus are not a mathematical solution; rather, they are a reflection of God's never-ending forgiveness. Nothing is beyond his forgiveness. So, whatever the sin of others against us, we are to forgive. We too are sinners.

It's not easy. Having endured the pain of her marriage, Ellen now suffered the discomfort of Jesus' command. Sinned against, we might also feel that we can't forgive. Maybe we feel condemned by our own inability to do so. You can probably think of those whose lives have been spoilt by the lifelong carrying of such hurt.

Remember God's love for us, Jesus on the cross and his Spirit who prays for us. We need the help of all three to forgive those who have wronged us. Strangely, when we take the pain of our 'unforgiveness' to him, our perspective is changed. There is a transforming freedom in forgiving others, knowing that the offence is in God's hands. Could you do that now?

■ PRAYER

'Our Father in heaven… forgive us our debts, as we also have forgiven our debtors' (Matthew 6:9, 12). Amen

Luke 7:37–38, 48–50 (NIV, abridged)

Who are the sinners?

A woman… who lived a sinful life learned that Jesus was eating at the Pharisee's house, so she came there with an alabaster jar of perfume. As she stood behind him at his feet weeping, she began to wet his feet with her tears. Then she wiped them with her hair, kissed them and poured perfume on them… Jesus said to her, 'Your sins are forgiven… Your faith has saved you; go in peace.'

I remember Carol, who hesitated at the church door, feeling she wasn't good enough to come in. Jeremy did come in, but as he listened, he decided that people here would condemn him. Distressed, he walked out of the church.

In Luke's story, a 'sinful' woman approaches Jesus. Imagine the horror of the party host – this woman, in my house! Imagine the feelings of the woman, faithfully hoping that Jesus would not reject her. She had no words, but instead poured out her life before him. Jesus knew her story and heard her unvoiced cry. 'Your faith has saved you,' he said.

The outraged host was shocked (v. 39). Forgiveness, he thought (presumably) wasn't for the likes of her! So, Luke's account asks us, 'Who are the sinners here?' Could Jesus even be pointing at us? The good news is that – whether we stand in the sinful woman's shoes, or are dressed in our best at a church event – Jesus accepts whoever comes to him, recognising their need of his forgiveness, and offers wholeness.

■ **PRAYER**

Lord Jesus, we are sorry that, sometimes, we turn others away from you. Thank you for your welcome and your forgiveness. Amen

Colossians 3:12b–14 (NIV)

Bind us together...

Clothe yourselves with compassion, kindness, humility, gentleness and patience. Bear with each other and forgive one another if any of you has a grievance against someone. Forgive as the Lord forgave you. And over all these virtues put on love, which binds them all together in perfect unity.

God's people we may be, but we're human – and we fall out with one another. The original grievance may seem minor (e.g. we don't like choices made about chairs for our church, we're offended by someone's comments about our reading), but the consequences of our minor disagreements can be major, threatening the unity of Christ's body in our local church. But there is a solution.

Clothed in Christlikeness, we are to 'forgive as the Lord forgave'. This should be our default setting. Putting aside critical attitudes, unkindness, pride, bombast and impatience (might you ever be guilty of such things?), we are to 'bear with each other', and work with Jesus in building unity through the overwhelming power of his love.

Take a few moments to think about your own faith community. Be honest, are you hanging on to a grievance against someone? How might the qualities the apostle Paul lists here change your attitude – and the situation? It's difficult to do on your own. Only Christ's love can bind us together in unity as his people.

■ **PRAYER**

Clothe me, Christ, in your love, and in Paul's words, bind us together in perfect unity. Amen

Luke 23:40–43 (NIV, abridged)

It's never too late

But the other criminal rebuked him. 'Don't you fear God?... We are punished justly, for we are getting what our deeds deserve. But this man has done nothing wrong.' Then he said, 'Jesus, remember me when you come into your kingdom.' Jesus answered him, 'Truly I tell you, today you will be with me in paradise.'

I've been bad... It's unfair to ask God's forgiveness now... Is it too late?

Suffering the excruciating Roman punishment for crime, this thief on the cross was at the end of his earthly life. Yet, somehow, he understood that Jesus was alongside him, enduring the same pain, but without crime. Nearing death, words and rational thinking about theology were not uppermost in his mind, but he knew and declared the truth about God's Son. Yes, I have done wrong, but this man is innocent. In Jesus there is hope: 'Remember me when you come into your kingdom.'

As Christians we sometimes impose rules on others or ourselves, which we believe make us right with God. You've got to understand the theology, speak the right words as evidence – but surely, all that was too late for this dying man? Look again at this story. He simply turns to Jesus, confesses his sin and trusts in the hope he sees in him. Out of such faith arises the joy of Jesus' response: 'Today you will be with me...'

■ **PRAYER**

It's not too late for any of us. Turn towards Jesus now: receive his love, forgiveness and life.

Luke 15:20–24 (NIV, abridged)

Coming home...

Still a long way off, his father saw him and was filled with compassion for him; he ran to his son, threw his arms round him and kissed him. The son said to him, 'Father, I have sinned against heaven and against you...' But the father said... 'Let's have a feast and celebrate. For this son of mine was dead and is alive again; he was lost and is found.'

Will he forgive me? Will he let me come back? Jesus' story of the return of the lost son gives us the answer. Even as we turn towards home, God our Father watches us on our journey. He knows our troubled lives and thoughts, he knows our shame – and he is filled with compassion for us. In fact, he runs towards us, embraces us and welcomes us. He names us as his child. Repentance has brought revolution; forgiveness brings joy and celebration.

But this isn't 'cheap grace'. The son acknowledged his sin, not only against his father, but also against God in heaven. He knew he was unworthy of forgiveness and was willing to do what he could to make amends (v. 19). But God's abundant grace isn't like that. It is freely given to those who turn to him – 'the gift of God' (Ephesians 2:8).

Feeling far from God? Our Father sees us. Let's not be afraid to come home to his embrace. He welcomes us – this is the good news of God's kingdom.

■ PRAYER

Father God, I have sinned against you (Luke 15:21). Thank you for your forgiveness and welcome. Amen

The hymn book of Israel

David Butterfield

For the last three years of my ministry before I retired, I served as a member of the clergy team at York Minster. At the start of the main Sunday service, it was wonderful to walk in procession down the centre aisle singing a hymn of worship like 'O praise ye the Lord' to the accompaniment of the Minster organ.

Music has always been important in Christian worship. In two of his letters, Paul encourages his readers to 'sing psalms, hymns and spiritual songs' (Colossians 3:16, NRSV; see also Ephesians 5:19). Back in Old Testament times music also played a significant part in the worship of God's people. Their 'hymn book' was the book of Psalms – the word 'psalm' means 'a song accompanied by a stringed instrument'. Many of them were written by King David, who was a gifted musician, and of the ten very different psalms I've chosen for these reflections, five were written by David.

The themes of the 150 psalms are varied. In some we praise God with great joy; in others we confess our sins to him. In some we rejoice in God's saving power; in others we express deep lament because of the difficult circumstances we are going through.

Space allows me only to include a verse or two from each psalm within each reflection, so if you have a Bible, I suggest that you read the whole psalm. I hope you enjoy reading this exploration of the psalms and that the words of the writers will speak into your life today.

Psalm 1:1–2a (NRSV)

A psalm in praise of God's word

Happy are those who do not follow the advice of the wicked or take the path that sinners tread or sit in the seat of scoffers, but their delight is in the law of the Lord.

In my retirement I have been making videos for a number of junior schools to use in their assemblies. As well as focusing on individual Bible stories, I have also produced a series which is a whistlestop tour of the Bible from Genesis to Revelation. As I have prepared these, I have become more and more aware of the importance of the scriptures.

In the very first psalm, the writer declares that we will be blessed if our 'delight is in the law of the Lord'. By 'the law of the Lord', the writer would have been referring to the 'Bible' of his day, which was probably the first five books of the Old Testament.

It's good for us to find a space each day when we can read our Bibles. With so many versions available, it's easy to find a translation that suits us. As a tree planted by the waterside will thrive, so we will be blessed when our delight is in the law of the Lord.

■ **PRAYER**
Heavenly Father, open my eyes that I may see wonderful things in your word. Amen

Psalm 118:1 (NIV)

A psalm of thanksgiving

Give thanks to the Lord, for he is good; his love endures forever.

It is very pleasing to receive a thank-you letter when you have given someone a gift. In our technological age, such thank-yous are probably more likely to be sent by mobile phone. Saying 'thank you' is important and is something most parents teach their children to do.

The writer of this psalm begins by exhorting us to 'give thanks to the Lord'. He then gives some reasons why he is thankful to God, and he relates how the Lord helped him when he was in some tight spots. We have a lot to be thankful for.

There's an old hymn that goes, 'Count your blessings, name them one by one, and it will surprise you what the Lord has done.' So, what are the blessings for which you should thank God? You could jot down a list of them and then make a point of saying 'thank you' to your heavenly Father.

■ **PRAYER**

Heavenly Father, thank you for all the good things you bless me with. May I always have a thankful heart. Amen

Psalm 8:1a, 4 (NIV)

A psalm in praise of God's majesty

Lord, our Lord, how majestic is your name in all the earth!… what is mankind that you are mindful of them, human beings that you care for them?

Back in the 1980s I became interested in astronomy. I bought a ten-inch reflecting telescope as well as some books on the subject. It was amazing to see the moons around Jupiter, the rings of Saturn and the Andromeda galaxy, which is 2.5 million light years away.

King David, the author of this psalm, was inspired when he looked up into the night sky. This was many centuries before the light pollution that unfortunately keeps us from seeing the true glory of the heavens at night. In this psalm of praise to God, David focuses on two aspects of the nature of God which are related. The first is how great and majestic he is to create the universe in all its vastness, its beauty and its complexity. The second is that, even though God is so great, he chooses to be 'mindful' of ordinary people like you and me.

So as you think about the majesty of God, remember also that he is 'mindful' of you and the circumstances of your life today.

■ **PRAYER**

Heavenly Father, thank you that even in all your majesty, you are mindful of me today. Amen

Psalm 15:1 (NIV)

A psalm of personal reflection

Lord, who may dwell in your sacred tent? Who may live on your holy mountain?

In Jane Austen's novel, *Sense and Sensibility*, as a young man, Edward Ferrars proposed to Lucy Steele and got engaged to her. Some years later, he developed an affection for the heroine of the story, Elinor Dashwood. However, because he was a man of principle, he would not break his promise to Lucy Steele even though, on reflection, he admitted that he had been foolish to propose to her. So he exemplifies great loyalty when he sacrifices his potential happiness with Elinor to honour the promise he made to Lucy. In the end, Lucy decides to marry Edward's younger brother Robert, who is a much richer man than Edward, so Edward is released from his oath and is able to marry Elinor.

In Psalm 15, King David challenges those who were worshipping at the temple in Jerusalem to make sure they were living godly lives. He lists eleven qualities that worshippers should display. One of them is a person 'who keeps an oath even when it hurts'. So Edward Ferrars would have ticked that box. Other qualities that are listed include telling the truth, not speaking ill against others and doing what is right. When we seek to come into God's presence, whether on our own or with others, it's important that we examine our hearts to see that we are living in a way that pleases God. Perhaps you could use this psalm as a checklist.

■ **PRAYER**

May the words of my mouth and the meditation of my heart be pleasing in your sight, Lord, my rock and my redeemer (see Psalm 19:14). Amen

Psalm 23:1 (GNT)

A psalm of trust

The Lord is my shepherd; I have everything I need.

My wife Irene and I enjoy walking in the countryside around Ripon where we live. On our walks we often encounter sheep and, in the spring, newborn lambs. Sheep farmers must ensure that their flocks are safe and secure and, as a shepherd, David knew how vulnerable sheep were to predators.

In the first half of the psalm, David recounts how he lived securely under God's shepherd-like care. His trust in God comes over clearly when he says, 'Even if I go through the deepest darkness, I will not be afraid, Lord, for you are with me. Your shepherd's rod and staff protect me.' It's easy to trust God when things are going well. It's not so easy when we feel that we are walking through 'the deepest darkness'. Yet it's in this verse that David changes from addressing God as 'he' to 'you' and, with great trust in God, he says: 'For you are with me'. This is a personal and relational God.

David continued to trust God was with him even in the darkest times. May his well-known words inspire us to continue to trust God through the dark times as well as through the good times.

■ **PRAYER**

Heavenly Father, thank you that I need fear no evil because you are with me. Amen

Psalm 136:1 (NIV)

A psalm in praise of God's salvation

Give thanks to the Lord, for he is good. His love endures forever.

I enjoy reading a good story last thing at night before I turn out the light. In Psalm 136, the writer tells a story – it's the story of how God saved his people from slavery in Egypt. He recounts how God divided the Red Sea and eventually brought his people into the promised land. The full stories are told in Exodus and Joshua. The first half of each verse of this psalm was probably sung by a cantor with the full congregation responding each time with: 'His love endures forever.'

The New Testament tells us another story – the story of the salvation that Jesus came to bring and how we can be saved from a different sort of slavery. As you look back on your life, what are the highlights of your Christian story? Can you think of times when you sensed God intervened in your life or guided you in a special way?

If you were to write a psalm about the journey of your life, what would you include? Why not jot down a few headings on a piece of paper, read through them and end with the final words of this psalm, 'Give thanks to the God of heaven. His love endures forever.'

■ **PRAYER**

Heavenly Father, thank you for the story of my life and for the way you have guided me and blessed me. Amen

Psalm 51:1a (NRSV)

A psalm of repentance

Have mercy on me, O God, according to your steadfast love.

One day, a prophet called Nathan visited King David and told him a story. It was about a rich man who had a very large number of sheep and cattle, but stole a lamb from a poor man. It was the only lamb he had. When David heard this, he was furious. At that moment Nathan said to him, 'You are the man!' His story was a parable that revealed how David had committed adultery with Bathsheba, who was married to Uriah. (You can read this story in 2 Samuel 12.) David was overcome with remorse and expressed his repentance by writing this psalm. He is completely honest with God. He doesn't make excuses; he simply owns up to his sin and, as a result, receives God's forgiveness.

As you look back on your life, can you think of anything you did or said that you deeply regret? Perhaps there may be times when such a memory comes back to you with a sense of unease. As Christians we are blessed to know, in a way that David didn't, that, as the hymn puts it, Jesus 'died that we might be forgiven'.

If there is something in the past which you feel you should confess to God, take a moment to do this with the same honesty as King David. Then, at the end of your prayer, imagine Jesus saying to you what he once said to a paralysed man, 'Your sins are forgiven.'

■ PRAYER

'Create in me a clean heart, O God, and put a new and right spirit within me' (Psalm 51:10). Amen

Psalm 93:1a (NIV)

A royal psalm

The Lord reigns, he is robed in majesty.

Did you watch the coronation service for King Charles III in May last year? A peak audience of about 20 million people in the UK watched the service and many more around the world. I was particularly impressed by the Christian content of the service and the inspiring music of Sir Hubert Parry's anthem 'I was glad' and Handel's 'Zadok the Priest'. Commenting on the grandeur and splendour of the occasion, my wife pointed out how we Brits do pageantry and ceremony so very well. The climax was when our newly crowned king was seated on the throne in Westminster Abbey.

In this psalm of enthronement, God's people of old imagine God being crowned as their king. The writer emphasises the power of their divine king as he declares that he is 'mightier than the thunder of the great waters' (v. 4) and 'robed in majesty and armed with strength' (v. 1). Even the thunder of the pounding waves is no match for the power of God.

This psalm can encourage us in at least two ways. First, we can have confidence that the God who watches over our lives is a mighty God and nothing is beyond his control. This means that we really can trust him to guide us through the challenges that sometimes come our way. A second encouragement is that, if God really is king, then we are to be his faithful and loyal servants, aiming to please him in all that we think, say and do.

■ PRAYER

Heavenly Father, thank you that I can have confidence that as king you hold me with your great power and might. Amen

Psalm 13:1 (NIV)

A psalm of lament

How long, Lord? Will you forget me forever? How long will you hide your face from me?

Like the writer of this psalm, during the long months of the coronavirus pandemic, many people across the world must have cried out, 'How long?' It's a question many of us may have asked as we yearned for life to get back to what we once knew.

This is the cry of King David in this psalm. Life has become so tough for him that he feels that God has forgotten him and is hiding from him. Many people go through times when God seems far away and so will be able to identify with David when he asked, 'How long must I… have sorrow in my heart?' (v. 2).

Having cried out to God in desperation at the start of this psalm, he concludes his lament with a prayer of faith. As a deliberate act of will, David chooses to trust God, to rejoice in his salvation and to sing the Lord's praise even amid his darkness and confusion.

Whenever we feel in a dark place, it's good to put our will into gear and praise God in faith. Many people have found that this really can sustain them through dark times.

■ **PRAYER**

Heavenly Father, I trust in your unfailing love. Dispel the darkness and give light to my eyes. Amen

Psalm 150:6a (NIV)

A psalm of praise

Let everything that has breath praise the Lord.

In my introduction to this series, I mentioned that the word 'psalm' means 'a song of praise'. The last psalm in 'the hymn book of Israel' ends, literally, on a high note as the writer exhorts everyone 13 times to praise God and to use a myriad of musical instruments.

I find it's all too easy for me to sing hymns and songs without giving adequate thought to the words. Yet, at other times I have found that the words of certain hymns and songs have really struck a chord with me. When that has happened, they have become vehicles for my worship as I have sung them with real meaning.

Can you think of some hymns or songs that mean a lot to you? If so, spend a moment reading through the words and imagining the music in your mind. Or, if you are confident using the technology, play them on your phone, tablet or computer and sing along with your lips or in your mind. In that way you will be responding to the psalmist's exhortation in the final verse: 'Let everything that has breath praise the Lord!'

■ PRAYER

Heavenly Father, thank you for the gift of music, and for instruments and voices that we can use to give you our praise. Amen

A friend indeed

I no longer call you servants, because a servant does not know his master's business. Instead, I have called you friends, for everything that I learned from my Father I have made known to you. You did not choose me, but I chose you and appointed you so that you might go and bear fruit – fruit that will last – and so that whatever you ask in my name the Father will give you.

JOHN 15:15–16 (NIV)

In this verse Jesus is speaking to his disciples in the upper room, a farewell and a sending out, words of comfort and empowerment to get them through the coming days. Here he makes it explicit, those gathered in the room are his friends. Their relationship has transcended that of master and servant through the sharing of knowledge. For a servant simply follows the orders of the master while a friend with profound understanding can take initiative and carry ideas forward – and ultimately bear lasting fruit.

For over 100 years, BRF Ministries has been working to share the knowledge of the gospel with as many people of all ages as possible – from Living Faith resources, such as our *Bible Reflections for Older People* reading notes, to the work of our other ministries: Anna Chaplaincy, Messy Church and Parenting for Faith. It is our goal not only to share the Bible but to give people the tools for deeper understanding and for building a friendship with God that they can then take forward and, in their own lives and communities, bear fruit.

Our work is made possible through kind donations from individuals, charitable trusts and gifts in wills. If you would like to support our work you can become a Friend of BRF by making a monthly gift of £2 a month or more – we thank you for your friendship.

Find out more at **brf.org.uk/donate** or get in touch with us on **01235 462305** or via **giving@brf.org.uk**.

Judith Moore
Fundraising development officer

Grandparenting brings new life and joy, and also the opportunity to walk spiritually alongside our grandchildren. In this book, Becky Sedgwick explores how grandparents can proactively encourage and equip their grandchildren to meet and know God, offering tools and skills for the journey. Whatever your circumstances, God has positioned you to be a unique voice speaking into your grandchildren's lives, helping to nurture them into the reality of a relationship with the God who loves them.

Grandparenting for Faith *(Publishing January 2024)*
Sharing God with the children you love the most
Becky Sedgwick
978 1 80039 204 5 £9.99
brfonline.org.uk

A 40-day journey exploring the themes of hope and new life through vivid biblical images, *Holding Onto Hope* can be used through Lent or during any 40-day period. We start with how all creation praises God and then explore the agricultural pattern of sowing, growing and harvesting before moving to the gracious promises and invitations God makes to his people. Next come images of God as our help and refuge. Finally, we focus on our new life in Christ.

Holding Onto Hope
40 days of God's encouragement through art and reflections
Amy Boucher Pye and Leo Boucher
978 1 80039 200 7 £12.99
brfonline.org.uk

To order

Online: brfonline.org.uk
Telephone: +44 (0)1865 319700
Mon–Fri 9.30–17.00
Post: complete this form and send to the address below

Delivery times within the UK are normally 15 working days. Prices are correct at the time of going to press but may change without prior notice.

Title	Issue	Price	Qty	Total
Grandparenting for Faith		£9.99		
Holding onto Hope		£12.99		
Bible Reflections for Older People (single copy)	Jan–Apr 2024	£5.50		
Bible Reflections for Older People (single copy)	May–Aug 2024	£5.55		

POSTAGE AND PACKING CHARGES			
Order value	UK	Europe	Rest of world
Under £7.00	£2.00		
£7.00–£29.99	£3.00	Available on request	Available on request
£30.00 and over	FREE		

Total value of books	
Donation	
Postage and packing	
Total for this order	

Please complete in BLOCK CAPITALS

Title .... First name/initials .... Surname.................................

Address ....

.... Postcode ....

Acc. No. .... Telephone ....

Email ....

Method of payment

❏ Cheque (made payable to BRF) ❏ MasterCard / Visa

Card no. ☐☐☐☐ ☐☐☐☐ ☐☐☐☐ ☐☐☐☐

Expires end ☐☐ ☐☐ Security code ☐☐☐ Last 3 digits on the reverse of the card

We will use your personal data to process this order. From time to time we may send you information about the work of BRF Ministries. Please contact us if you wish to discuss your mailing preferences **brf.org.uk/privacy**

Registered with
FUNDRAISING
REGULATOR

Please return this form to:
BRF Ministries, 15 The Chambers, Vineyard, Abingdon OX14 3FE | **enquiries@brf.org.uk**
For terms and cancellation information, please visit brfonline.org.uk/terms.

Bible Reading Fellowship is a charity (233280) and company limited by guarantee (301324), registered in England and Wales

BIBLE REFLECTIONS FOR OLDER PEOPLE **GROUP SUBSCRIPTION FORM**

> All our Bible reading notes can be ordered online
> by visiting **brfonline.org.uk/subscriptions**

The group subscription rate for *Bible Reflections for Older People* will be £16.65 per person until April 2025.

☐ I would like to take out a group subscription for .... (*quantity*) copies.

☐ Please start my order with the May 2024 / September 2024 / January 2025* issue.
(*delete as appropriate*)

Please do not send any money with your order. Send your order to BRF Ministries and we will send you an invoice.

Name and address of the person organising the group subscription:

Title .... First name/initials .... Surname..

Address..

.... Postcode ....

Telephone .... Email ....

Church..

Name and address of the person paying the invoice if the invoice needs to be sent directly to them:

Title .... First name/initials .... Surname..

Address..

.... Postcode ....

Telephone .... Email ....

Please return this form to:
BRF Ministries, 15 The Chambers, Vineyard, Abingdon OX14 3FE | **enquiries@brf.org.uk**
For terms and cancellation information, please visit brfonline.org.uk/terms.

Bible Reading Fellowship is a charity (233280) and company limited by guarantee (301324), registered in England and Wales

BIBLE REFLECTIONS FOR OLDER PEOPLE INDIVIDUAL/GIFT SUBSCRIPTION FORM

To order online, please visit **brfonline.org.uk/subscriptions**

☐ I would like to take out a subscription (*complete your name and address details only once*)
☐ I would like to give a gift subscription (*please provide both names and addresses*)

Title .... First name/initials .... Surname...

Address..

....Postcode ....

Telephone.................................Email...

Gift subscription name ....

Gift subscription address ....

....Postcode..........................

Gift message (*20 words max. or include your own gift card*):

....

....

Please send **Bible Reflections for Older People** beginning with the May 2024 / September 2024 / January 2025* issue (**delete as appropriate*):

(*please tick box*) | **UK** | **Europe** | **Rest of world**
Bible Reflections for Older People | ☐ £21.15 | ☐ £28.35 | ☐ £32.40

Total enclosed £ .... (*cheques should be made payable to 'BRF'*)

Please charge my MasterCard / Visa with £ ....

Card no. ☐☐☐☐ ☐☐☐☐ ☐☐☐☐ ☐☐☐☐

Expires end ☐☐☐☐ M M Y Y   Security code ☐☐   Last 3 digits on the reverse of the card

We will use your personal data to process this order. From time to time we may send you information about the work of BRF Ministries. Please contact us if you wish to discuss your mailing preferences **brf.org. uk/privacy**

Please return this form to:
BRF Ministries, 15 The Chambers, Vineyard, Abingdon OX14 3FE | **enquiries@brf.org.uk**
For terms and cancellation information, please visit brfonline.org.uk/terms.

Bible Reading Fellowship is a charity (233280) and company limited by guarantee (301324), registered in England and Wales